Icky Ice Cream:
A Short Sweet Story of Brief Best Friends

Laura Hoffenberg
Illustrated by: Jessica Gamboa

Dedicated to Mr. McAteer.
I promised I wouldn't forget him when I published my first children's book.

I went to Pinky's Pet Store at noon just yesterday.

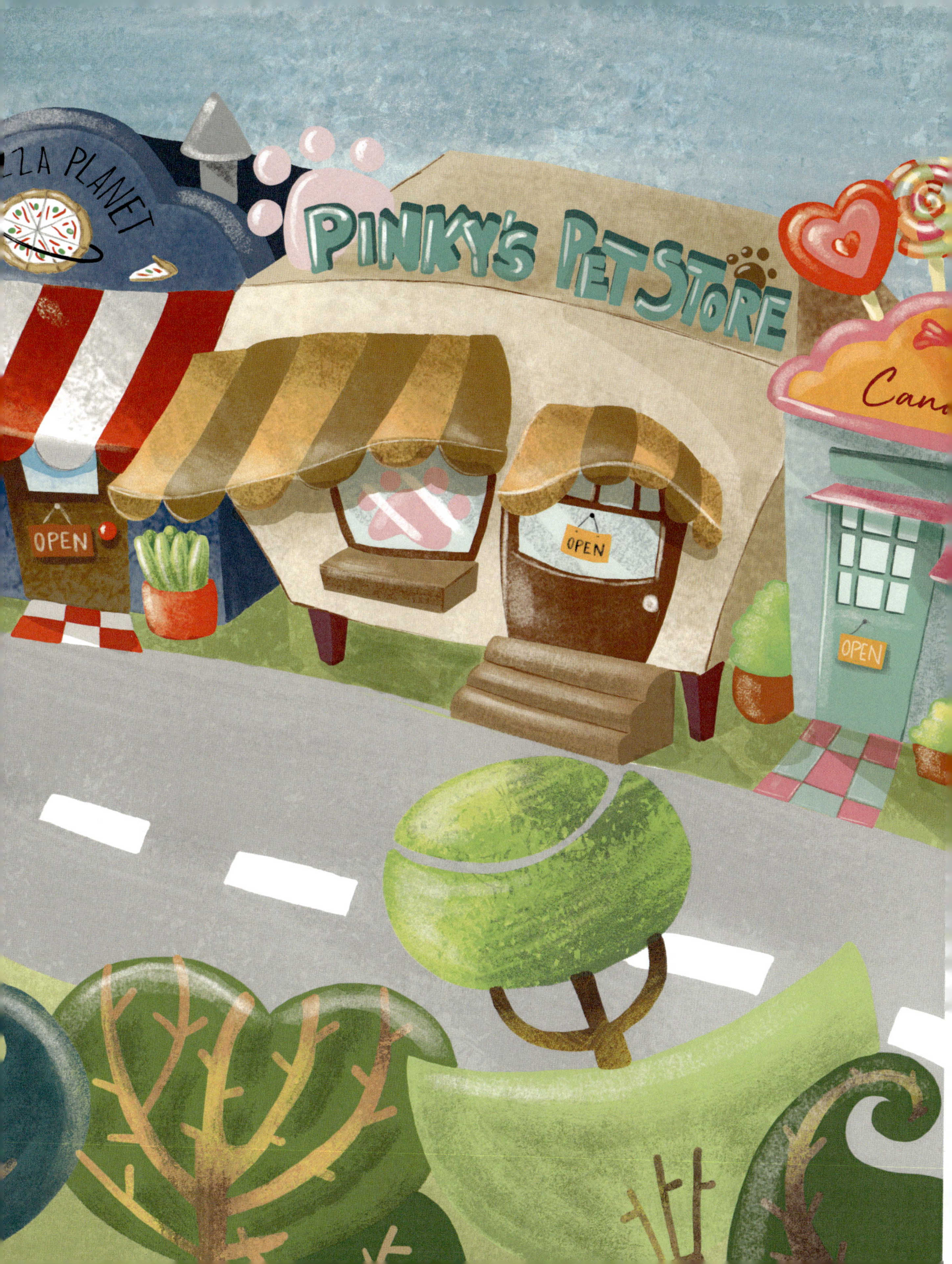
ZZA PLANET
PINKY'S PET STORE
OPEN
OPEN
OPEN
Can

I'd kicked

and screamed

and faked a croak,

'til I finally got my way.

Mum said not too big,
or stinky, hairy, gross,

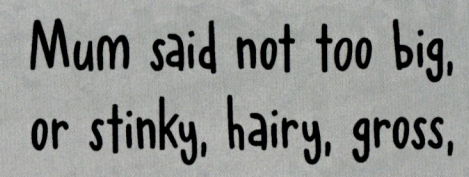

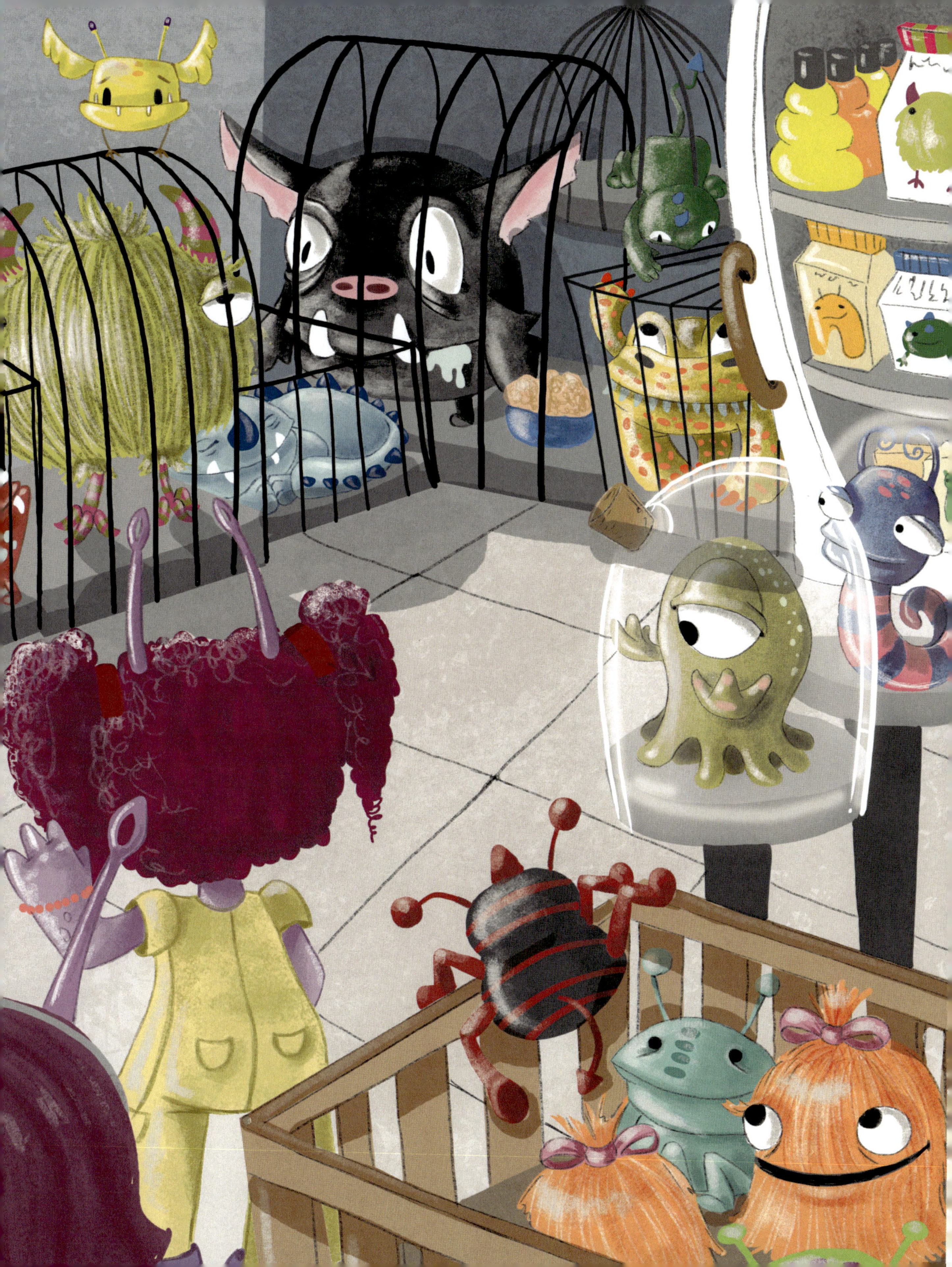

and that's when I saw Princess,

my new albino cockroach.

She was the perfect pet;
never whined or wet the bed.

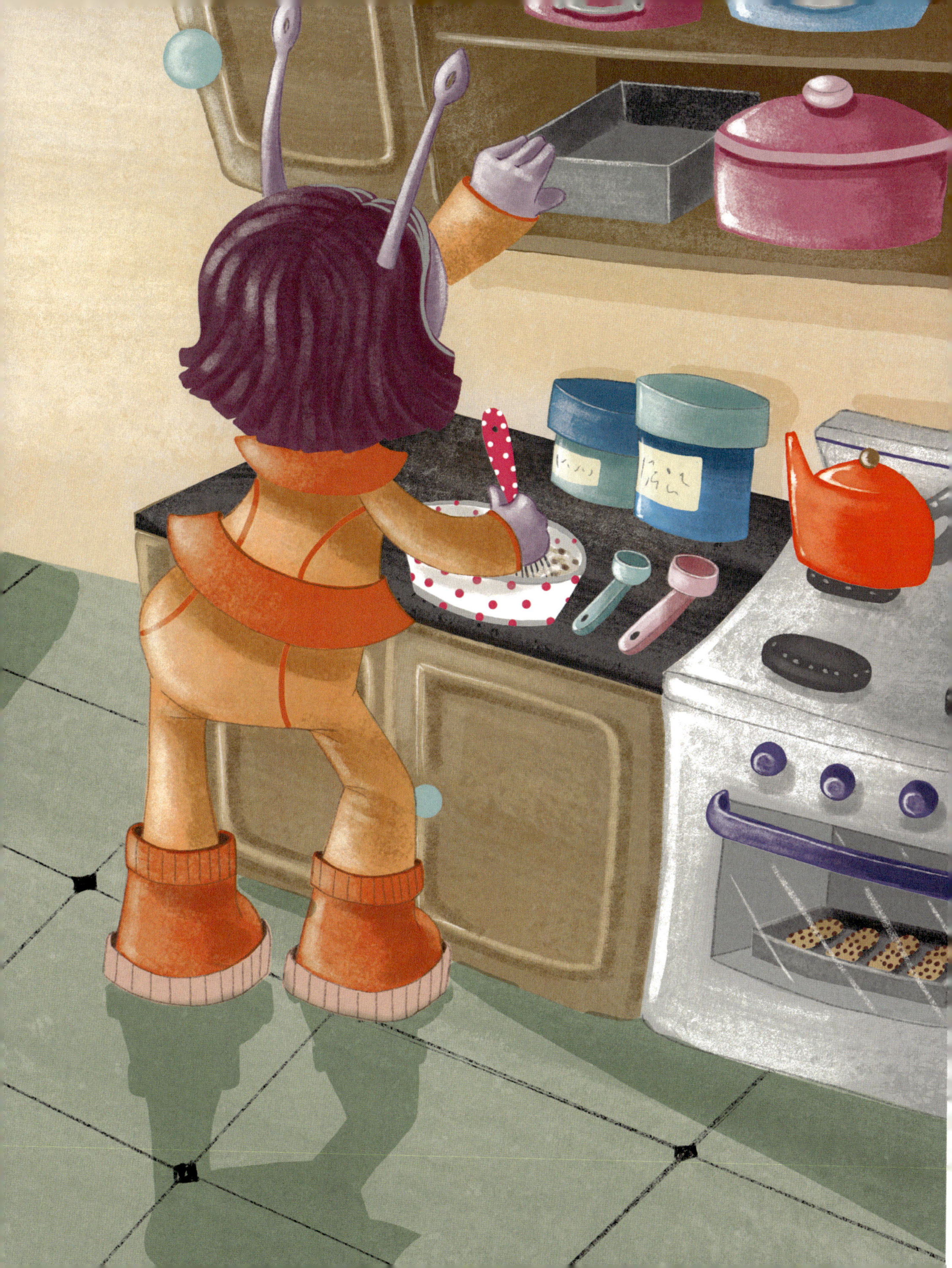

I let her share my pillow,

and she snuggled near my head.

I kept her in my pocket while climbing every tree,

explorers and best friends,

darling Princess and me.

She was the perfect pet,
always listened to my woes.

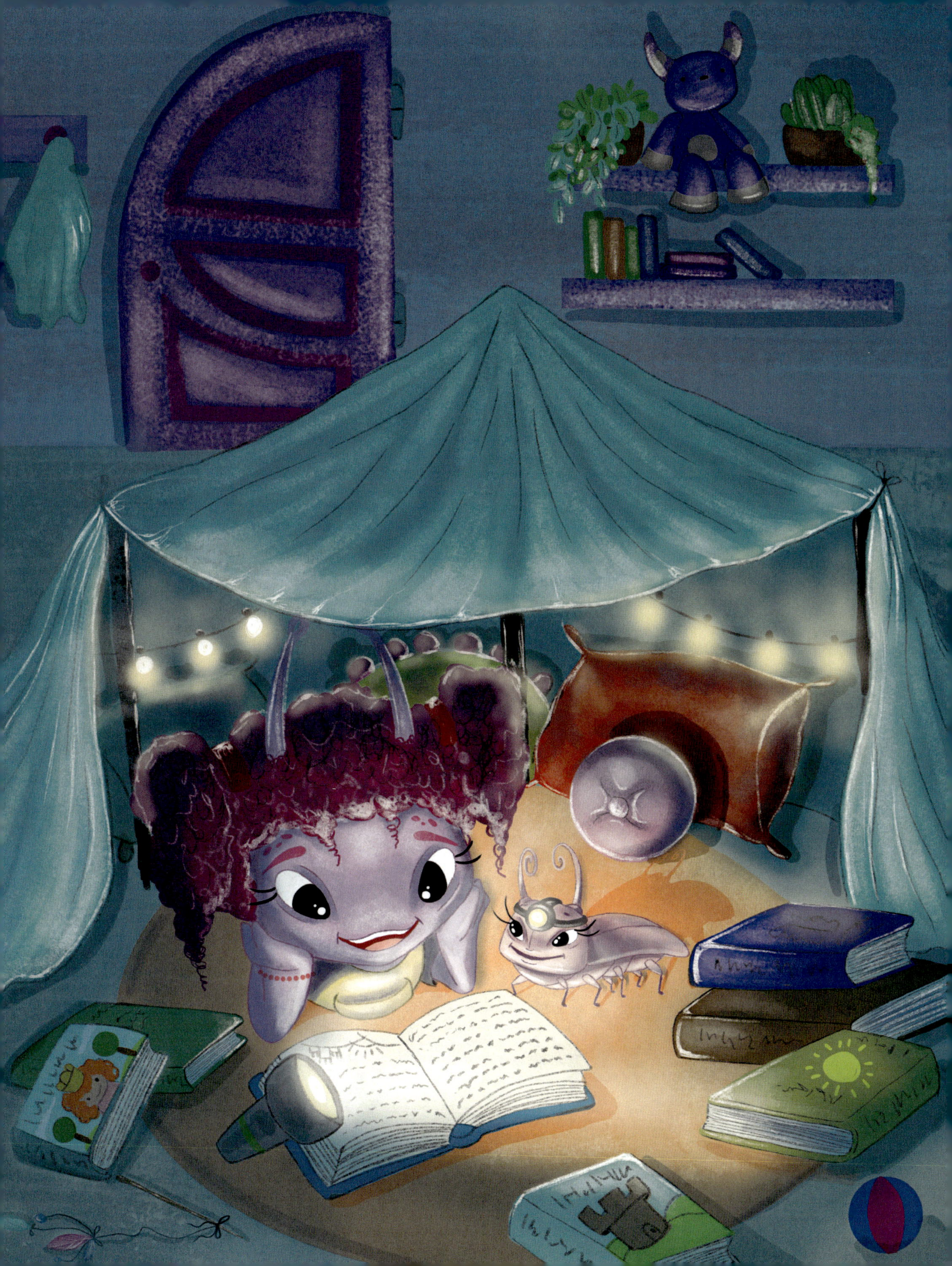

But one day I stepped too soon,

and she got caught beneath my toes.

There was a *squish,*

SQUISH

a horrible *splat—*

SPLAT

AHHHHHH

I thought I heard a scream...

and before I knew it,
Princess had turned

into vanilla ice cream.

Our friendship was short but sweet,
one I'll remember for all of time.

The briefest of best friends, darling Princess, and I.

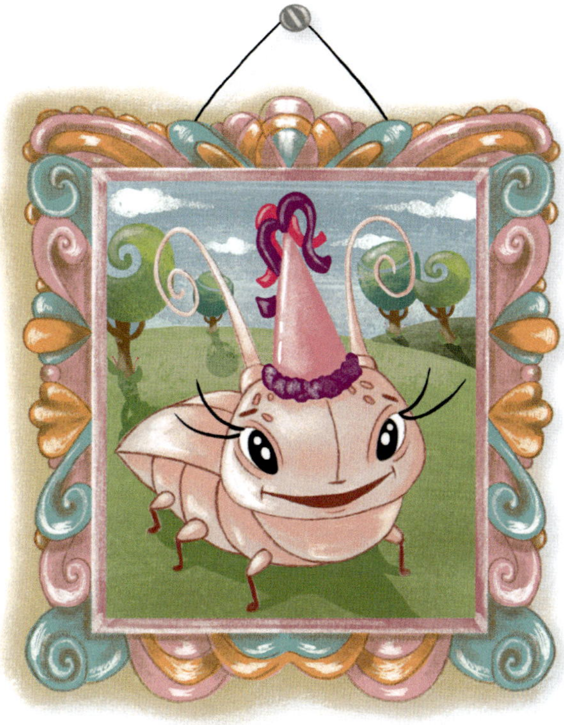

Laura Hoffenberg has been writing children's poems since the day she found "Kids Pick the Funniest Poems", a collection edited by Bruce Lansky, on her childhood bookshelf. It was the first time she'd ever read a poem that could make her belly-laugh...and it made her extremely glad her nose was on her face!

Adapting one of her own favorites into a children's book has been a long-time dream. She hopes that it can bring just as many smiles to kids' faces as that first book brought to hers.
She currently resides in NYC with her husband and their cat, Olive.

Made in the USA
Middletown, DE
14 December 2023